Harry Kernell

Harry Kernell

ISBN/EAN: 9783744794664

Printed in Europe, USA, Canada, Australia, Japan

Cover: Foto ©Thomas Meinert / pixelio.de

More available books at **www.hansebooks.com**

HARRY KERNELL'S
"ECCENTRIC IRISH"
SONGSTER.

CONTAINING THE VERY ESSENCE OF IRISH WIT AND HUMOR IN THE
FORM OF JOLLY, CHARACTERISTIC, LUDICROUS, COMIC, AND SEMI-
COMIC HIBERNIAN SONGS AND BALLADS, AS SUNG TO IM-
MENSE AND RAPTUROUS AUDIENCES BY THE IMITATIVE
BUT INIMITABLE

HARRY KERNELL,
The Champion Irish Singing Humorist.

INCLUDING ALSO THE ORIGINAL SKETCH, WITH MUSIC, ENTITLED

" THE WHISTLING THIEF."

TO WHICH ARE ADDED

*THE FOLLOWING FOUR PIECES SET TO MUSIC EX-
PRESSLY FOR THIS WORK:*

A VIRGIN ONLY 19 YEARS OLD, Composed by HARRY RICKARDS.

THE SCAMP,   Composed by LANCE MAJOR.

UP A TREE,   Composed by HARRY CLIFTON.

ALL THE WORLD AROUND,   Composed by R. P. STEWART.

CONTENTS

OF

HARRY KERNELL'S "ECCENTRIC IRISH" SONGSTER.

☞ The Music of all the songs in this book can be obtained at any music store in the United States or Canada.

OPINIONS OF THE PRESS.

Mr. Harry Kernell, in the North of Ireland dialect, his anecdotes, songs and dances, is an original piece of business, and has no successful imitator.—*Louisville (Ky.) Paper.*

One of the really first-class features was the Irish dialect of Mr. Kernell.—*Chicago Evening Post.*

Harry Kernell introduces an entirely new feature in the variety business, and merits the many encores he receives.—*Minneapolis (Mo.) Paper.*

One of the greatest features of the entertainment was Harry Kernell, who sung, danced, and talked in the North of Ireland dialect until his auditors were fairly aching at the sides from laughing. He retired amid much cheering.—*Ottawa (Ca.) Paper.*

Mr. Harry Kernell making his Obeisance.—This gentleman is the most accomplished Irish comedian we have ever seen—having the brogue and accent to perfection, though he has never seen the "Dear little Isle." In fact, he takes pride in claiming another nationality. He kept the house in a continuous roar of laughter.—*Montreal Canada.*

Last, not least, a new candidate for public favor has made a decided hit. Mr. Harry Kernell is a more than average representative of the rare North of Ireland comedian; and dances better than any of the leading men in his line.—*Cincinnati Enquirer.*

Harry Kernell, who sings, dances, and talks in the North of Ireland dialect, is very funny.—*Baltimore Paper.*

Harry Kernell is original, and everybody liked him.—*Washington Paper.*

Mr. Harry Kernell is the best stage Irishman we have ever seen. His ebulitions of humor seem to be the natural overflow of a joyous spirit, and not the studied gags so common to the stage, to laugh at which requires a painful effort on the part of the hearer. We have often sat and witnessed attempted portrayals of the characteristics of different nations, and have felt in duty bound to laugh. We went to be amused, and felt that the privilege of laughing was included in the price of admission; but every muscle in our face was pained in the effort to fulfill our obligation. In witnessing *Kernell's Irish Comicalities,* the inclination to laughter was spontaneous and irresistible, and the only pain we experienced was in the endeavor to control our risibilities.—*Phila. Sunday Mercury, May* 10, 1875.

But next to Tony Pastor, Mr. Harry Kernell—a North of Ireland comedian—provoked more mirth and immoderate laughter than any of his fellow performers. He has the accent beautifully, imitates the actions of his subject well, and rolls out an immense volume of witty sayings.—*Ottawa (Ca.) Paper.*

Harry Kernell, in his ten minutes of fun and laughter, made the audience roar.—*Toronto, (Ca.) Paper.*

Mr. Harry Kernell, Negro comedian, made his first appearance, and made a decided hit. He is equal to any in his line of specialties that ever appeared here. His dialect imitations of the old darkey at camp-meeting were perfection, and brought down the house.—*Syracuse Standard.*

Harry Kernell is the favorite of the troupe, receiving round after round of applause as he goes through his songs, dances, and imitations.—*Pittsburgh Evening Leader.*

Mr. Harry Kernell was particularly well received, his Irish character sketches convulsing the audience with laughter, and bringing down the house in storms of applause. He is the best in his line ever seen in Baltimore.—*Baltimore Evening News.*

Harry Kernell proved himself a splendid Irish comedian, and a fine dancer.—*Cincinnati Enquirer.*

Tony Pastor, Gus Williams, and Harry Kernell, are the big favorites of the audience.—*Phila. Evening Item, Aug.* 27, 1875.

Harry Kernell is as comical in his sketches as it is possible to be.—*Boston Post.*

But one of all who took down the house, was Harry Kernell, in North of Ireland talking and singing. His make up, dialect, and action were true to the life, and one of the most droll characterizations we have ever witnessed.—*Meriden (Conn.) Standard.*

Harry Kernell should devote himself entirely to Irish characters; there is no finer stage Irishman in the variety business than he.—*Pittsburgh Evening Leader.*

CLARENCE McGOWAN'S TROUBLES.

AIR.—"Sold Everywhere."

Sung by HARRY KERNELL.

HERE I am, an Irishman,
From Ireland I came;
I landed in America,
And here I will remain.
I had to struggle hard at first,
And I don't think it was fair—
No matter what I tried to do,
I was sold everywhere.

SPOKEN.—No matter what I tried to do, I couldn't get along.
I once opened a cheap music store; a fellow came in one day
and asked far a ballad called "Act on the Square, Boys;" and
I turned my back to him to get it, when he stole a four dollar
fiddle, and ran out. I took my girl to a party once, and at the
supper table I asked her if she liked cod-fish balls? She said
she didn't, nor she never attended one. But it's the same story,
I was—

CHORUS.

Sold, sold, everywhere,
Alas! I have been sold;
Sold here, sold there,
The half has not been told.
Sold right, sold left—
It ain't no use to try.
No matter what I try to do,
I am sold everywhere.

I went out once to a menagerie,
To see the animals jump;
When a monkey came bouncing out of a cage
And gave me an awful thump.
I immediately grabbed him by the tail,
His tail it then came loose;
And a little boy was standing by,
Said, "Glue it on, you goose!"

SPOKEN.—I couldn't glue it on, and I was arrested for cruelty
to orphans. I worked for a man once—the meanest man I ever
saw. He was so mean, he used to talk through his nose, afraid
of wearing his mouth out. He was so mean, he got married on
tick; and he has been living on tick ever since. He got on a
steamboat once, and when the captain came around to collect
the fare, he jumped overboard. He walked ashore in fifteen feet
of water. He was such a sponger he drew the water all up, and
walked clean ashore. Once he hired two Chinamen to blast

(1)

CLARENCE McGOWAN'S TROUBLES.—Concluded.

rocks. They put in too much powder, and the rocks blasted them fifteen feet up in the air. When they came down, he took it out of their wages for the time that they were up.

Sold, sold, etc.

> Wherever I go, I am bound
>   To pluck misfortune's bitter fruits;
> And find myself sold everywhere,
>   Except about the boots.
> Come, Fortune, turn your wheel again,
>   And be a little fair;
> And give a good turn for one
>   Who's been sold everywhere.

Sold, sold, etc.

STARS IN DE SKY.

BURLESQUE CAMP-MEETING SONG.

Written and sung by HARRY KERNELL.

> GABRIEL, blow dat silver horn,
>   Oh, my hallaleyah!
> We beat the debbil, sure as you're born;
>   Oh, my hallaleuah!
> We are going to glory by-and-by,
>   Oh, my hallaleuah!
> We will meet de angels near the sky.
>   Oh, my hallaleuah!

CHORUS.

> De railroad train am passing through,
> De world am getting out of view;
> The sisters dey am going, too!
> I will meet you by-and-by—by-and-by.
> Every star in de sky had a number,
> Number one, number two, number three;
> Good Lord, by-and-by—by-and-by.
> Good Lord, by-and-by.

> What makes the debbil hate me so?
>   Oh, my hallaleuah!
> He had a hold on me, but he let me go,
>   Oh, my hallaleuah!
> So look out, sisters, and bar in mind,
>   Oh, my hallaleuah!
> If he does catch you, he won't treat you kind,
>   Oh, my hallaleuah!

De railroad, etc.

(2)

SONG AND DANCE.

AIR.—" Martha Jane Barew."

Written for HARRY KERNELL by E. McCURDY.

THERE was a man named Pat McCann,
He courted a girl named Mary Ann,
He loved her very dearly, yes, he loved her as his life,
He dressed so gay on Patrick's day—
He popped the question right away—
And asked this little darling if she would be his wife;
Oh, to cry then she began right before this handsome man ;
" Arrah," says she, " you're the biggest blarney
I met in all my life," said Mary Ann to Pat McCann ;
" Go away from me, you naughty man,
Or else I will tell my mother, and she'll surely have your life."

CHORUS.

Oh, handsome Pat McCann loved his purty Mary Ann,
Every evening he would take her out a-walking,
He would buy her an oyster stew and molasses candy,
And the way he used to kiss her was so shocking.

Said Pat McCann to Mary Ann, " You are my darling jewel,
And if you will not accept my hand I'll go and end my life."
Said Mary Ann to Pat McCann,
" I love you more th▓▓any man,
And rather than refuse your hand I'll be your loving wife."
h, he bought her then the ring,
And many another purty thing ; he bought her silks and satins
Enough to last her life ; and although it was Lent
To church they went to ask the father
For his consent to marry this loving couple,
And make them man and wife.
                              Oh, handsome Pat, etc.

Now Pat McCann and Mary Ann
Are as happy as salt water clams ;
The divil a couple in all the land
With hearts so full of joy, for some time last spring
A little thing dropped in one day to hear Pat sing,
It's nice to be the father of a bouncing baby boy ;
Now they're like turtle doves,
They are happy in their loves,
All cares and sorrows are unknown, all troubles they defy ;
I wish my name was Pat McCann,
You would be my Mary Ann ;
I would hug and kiss you, darling, and be married by and by.
                              Oh, handsome Pat, etc.

THE O'SHAUGHNESSY GUARDS.

Written by WILLIAM WELCH.

As sung by Miss ADAH RICHMOND and HARRY KERNELL.

Two brave boys in our new uniform,
   Proud are we when we shoulder our guns;
We see flags and banners floating,
   As we go marching down Broadway.
           Then right face about. (*Symp.*)

CHORUS.

   Then we hear the drums a-beating,
   And the music sweetly play,
   As we go marching down Broadway
   Upon St. Patrick's day-ay-ay!
   We are out on a parade do you see,
   Cousin Mike and me—
   We'll march away, we'll march all day,
   Come and join our company.

The beautiful girls all throng the sidewalk,
   And wave their hands to our company;
They always throw us wreaths and bouquets,
   And give three cheers for Biddy and I.
         Then right face about.
             Then we hear, etc.

Now come, all young men, that's fond of fighting,
   And roll your names in our company;
All sorrows and woes we'll send a-kiting,
   And fight for fun and liberty.
             Then we hear, etc.

WHY DON'T YOU HIRE A HALL?

By George S. Knight.

I came out here when very small,
  The time I don't know when,—
At first I did not know so much,
  But I'm smarter now than then ;
I keep a liquor store down town,
  Where all the boys did meet,
And the funny things to me they said
  To you now I'll repeat.

CHORUS.

Why don't you hire a hall ?
  Oh, say go shoot that hat—
I commence to think you are too fresh ;
  Go jump in some salt vat,—
Don't talk us all to death ;
  Oh, tumble, do now, Ned,—
Cheese it now—give us a rest—
  Swim out, you're over your head.

I soon commenced to see and know
  What everything they meant,
And that the business didn't pay,
  I couldn't make a cent ;
So then I put my foot right down,
  I likewise told my clerk
To tell them fellows when they'd come
  That business wouldn't work.
                        Why don't you, etc.

THE ORIGIN OF IRELAND.

COMIC RECITATION.

WITH due condescension I'd call your attention
  To what I shall mention of Erin so green,
And without hesitation I'll show how that nation
  Became of creation the gem and the queen.

'Twas early one morning without any warning
  That Vanus was born in the beautiful sea,
And by the same token and sure 'twas provoking,
  Her pinions were soaking and wouldn't give play.

Old Neptune, who knew her, began to pursue her,
  In order to woo her—the wicked old Jew—
And almost had caught her, a top of the water,
  Great Jupiter's daughter, which never would do.

But Jove, the great Janus, looked down and saw Vanus,
  And Neptune so hainous pursuing her wild,
And he spoke out in thunder, he'd rend him asunder,
  And sure 'twas no wonder for chasing his child.

A star that was flying hard by him espying,
  He caught with small trying, and down let it snap;
It fell quick as winking on Neptune a-sinking,
  And gave him I'm thinking a bit of a rap.

That star it was dry land, both lowland and highland,
  And formed a sweet island the land of my birth;
Thus plain is the story, that sent down from glory,
  Old Erin asthore is the gem of the earth.

Upon Erin nately jumped Vanus so stately,
  But fainted kase lately so hard she was pressed,
Which much did bewilder, but ere it had killed her,
  Her father distilled her a drop of the best.

That sup was victorious, it made her feel glorious,
  A little uproarious I fear it might prove;
So how can you blame us that Ireland's so famous
  For drinking and beauty, for fighting and love.

JAR DOWN EVERYBODY.

End song, sung by HARRY KERNELL.

I saw a jay bird on a limb,
I turned around and winked at him,
I took my gun and aimed at him,
Shot him in de leg, left de marrow on de limb.

CHORUS (*Repeat.*)

Over in de Monegeholo,
Over in de Allegahnny,
Jar down everybody, everybody jar down,
Jar down every body, jar, jar, jar down.

I had a horse, his name was Jack,
I rode his tail to save his back ;
Oh, how that horse would rear and kick,
I coaxed him along with a hickory stick.
    Over in de Monegeholo, etc.

Bullfrog dressed in soldier's clothes,
Went down to the riber to shoot some crows,
Crows smelt powder and dey flew away,
Bullfrog he was mad dat day.
    Over in de Monegeholo, etc.

I AM SO GLAD.

A BURLESQUE CAMP-MEETING SONG.

Sung by HARRY KERNELL.

I am so glad, I am so glad,
When the old ship Zion was passing by,
I am so glad, oh, you will land on de Canaan shore !
You rise up in de morning,
And you look up yonder in de sky ;
And dere you see the eagle's nest,
And yar de young ones cry ;
I am so glad you git to glory by-and-by.
If you get over to Jordan,
 And you don't see me over dar ;
Send me a ring for a token of your love,
 Likewise a lock of your hair.
I look way over yonder,
 And what you 'spect I see ?
A great big angel on de boom of a ship,
 A beckoning along to me.
I am so glad,
 You get to Jordan by-and-by !

THE WHISTLING THIEF.

A SKETCH FOR TWO OR THREE CHARACTERS.

[*Scene, a cabin, window open. Chair, table, &c. If necessary, the character of the old lady may be personated by* PAT.
*A dress thrown over his costume, and a cap, which can be easily
removed, may complete his attire.*]

[*Enter* MARY, *singing.*]

When Pat comes over the hill, his colleen for to see,
His whistle, loud and shrill, the signal was to be.
"O Mary!" my mother cries, "there's somebody whistling,
    sure."
"No, mother, its only the wind, that's whistling through the
    door,
      That's whistling through the door."

[PAT, *outside, whistles* "Garry Owen."]

MARY (*listening*).—Oh, that's the dear boy. Now if I only
can keep him here unbeknown to my mother.

[*Enter the* MOTHER, *with a crutch.*]

MOTHER.—Mary dear. Mary, I say. Where are you?
MARY.—Here, mother dear. What is it you're after want-
ing with me?
MOTHER.—Didn't I hear somebody whistling, Mary?
MARY.—Sure, it was the wind, mother.

MOTHER *sings.*

I've lived a long time, Mary, in this wide world, my dear;
But the wind to whistle a tune like that I never before did
    hear.

MARY *sings.*

But, mother, you know the fiddle hangs just behind the
    chink,
And the wind upon the strings of it is playing a tune, I
    think;
    Is playing a tune, I think.

(1)

THE WHISTLING THIEF.—[Continued.]

[PAT, *outside, barks like a dog.*]

MOTHER *sings.*

The dog is barking now, and a fiddle can't play a tune.

MARY *sings.*

But, mother, you know that dogs will bark when they see
the moon.

MOTHER *sings.*

But how can he see the moon, when you know he's old and
blind ;
Blind dogs can't see the moon, nor fiddles be played by the
wind,
Nor fiddles be played by the wind.

[PAT, *outside, imitates a pig.*]

MOTHER *sings.*

And there now is the pig, oneasy in his mind.

MARY *sings.*

But, mother, you know the saying, that pigs can see the
wind.

MOTHER *sings.*

That's all very well in the day, but allow me, miss, to re-
mark
That pigs, no more than ourselves, can see anything in the
dark,
Can see anything in the dark.

MOTHER.—So, so, my daughter; get out wid your excuses.
You can't decave your ould mother.
MARY.—But, mother dear.
MOTHER.—Oh, go 'long wid ye.

MOTHER *sings.*

I'm not such a fool as ye think, I know very well it is Pat.
·   [*Goes to window.*]
Get out, ye whistling thief, and get along home out of that ;

(2)

And you, miss, be off to your bed; don't bother me wid youɪ
tears;
For though I've lost my eyes, I haven't yet lost my ears,
I haveu't yet lost my ears.

[*Exit* Mother, *shaking her crutch at* Mary.]

Pat (*at window*).—Whist, Mary mavourneen! Darlint, ar● you there?
Mary.—Yes, Pat; but be aisy, me mother is wide awake.
Pat.—Oh, bad luck to her—I mane, God bless the ould woman. [*Climbs through window.*]
Mary.—Oh, I know she'll hear us. If she does, sure she'll be after breaking every bone in your body.
Pat.—What do you suppose I'd care for that?
Mary.—Don't come whistling round the door any more, Pat. You ought to know better.
Pat.—Sure, I'll whistle now if you don't stop me mouth wid a kiss from those rosy lips of yours.
Mary.—Oh, go along wid yer blarney.
Pat.—Well, if you won't give me one I'll stale it. [*Kisses her.*]
Mother (*outside*).—Mary, Mary, come in; what kapes yeɪ so long? Do you want me to come and fetch yer? It's bed-time an hour ago, sure.
Mary.—Pat, go quick!
Pat.—Bedad, I will. Good-bye, darlint. [*Kisses her.*] I'll go outside the same way I came in. [*Jumps through the win-dow.*]
Mary.—I'm coming, mother dear.

[*Enter* Mother.]

Mother.—Is it all night you'd be after staying up? Come, along, yer ungrateful girl. Sure, yer head's so full of that whistling thief, Pat, that yer can't rest. Get in wid yer.
Mary.—Yes, mother. [*Kisses hand at window.*]

[*Exit* Mother *and* Mary.]

Pat (*leaning on window-sill*).—When I oome again, bedad, I'll come wid a still tongue in my head. Take my advice:

(3)

THE WHISTLING THIEF.—[Continued.]

PAT *sings*.

Now, boys, don't courting go too near to the house, d'ye mind;
Unless you're certain sure the old woman's both *deaf* and
blind ;
The days when they were young, forget they never can,
They're able to tell the difference 'twixt a fiddle, pig, dog
and a man ;
A fiddle, pig, dog and a man.

THE WHISTLING THIEF.

Lively..

Mary.

When Pat comes o - ver the hill, his

col - leen for to see, His whis - tle, loud and

shrill, the sig - nal was to be. "O

Ma - ry ! " my moth - er cries, "there's some-bod-y

whist - ling sure." "No, moth-er, it's on - ly the

(4)

THE WHISTLING THIEF.—[Concluded.]

wind   that's whist - ling through the   door,   That's

whistling thro' the door.

Garry Owen—*To be whistled or played after 1st verse.*

*The complete music of "*The Whistling Thief*," with the Piano Accompaniment, is published by* Oliver Ditson & Co., *277 Washington Street, Boston. Price, 30 Cents.*

(5)

THE BOULEVARD.

A POPULAR IRISH SONG.

The Music of this song is published by E. H. Harding, 229 Bowery, New York.   Price 10 cents.

As sung by John Roach.

Good evening to you, one and all,
   You're looking well I see ;
I took a trip in a great big ship
   Acrooss the raging sea ;
I've been out of work a month or more,
   And you know it's very hard ;
But now I've got a job to do
   Beyant on the Boulevard.

CHORUS.

   Whist I ad id-y ! whist I ad-i-d-y !
   Times are very hard,
   But now I've got a job to do
   Beyant on the Boulevard.

So here I am, an Irishman,
   And to work I'm not afraid ;
While my son does carry the pick, my boys
   And I do handle the spade;
My Uncle Dan is an Alderman,
   And he holds a grip in the ward ;
'Tis him that gives the tickets out
   To work on the Boulevard.
               Whist I ad-i-dy! etc.

So now farewell, I'm going away,
   I can no longer stay ;
For if I sing any more for you
   I'll lose a half a day ;
I'm going down to the City Hall,
   To try and get a card
To put my father's uncle to work
   Beyant on the Boulevard.
               Whist I ad-i-dy ! etc.

"I'M WHAT YOU CALL A MILITARY MAN!"

Entered according to Act of Congress, in the year 1874, by E. H. Harding, in the Office of the Librarian of Congress, Washington, D. C.

The Music of this song is published by E. H. Harding, 288 Bowery, New York. Price 10 cents.

Written and Composed by Geo. H. Hart.

I'm what you call a military man,
If you doubt me, I will prove it, for I can.
I stand just six foot two, " sans " a stocking or a shoe,
And a finer soldier you will never scan.

CHORUS.

To a " right shoulder shift," my musket I will lift,
And all the pretty faces I will scan, oh,
When the band does sweetly play, we will march, march away,
For I'm what you call a military man.

Whenever I go out upon parade,
I awaken in the breast of every maid,
A feeling they admire, for I set their heart on fire,
And of military men, they're not afraid.
        To a " right shoulder shift," etc.

When they see me marching proudly down Broadway,
They look at one another, and they say,
" Oh, what a splendid man, just look at him, Mary Ann,
I can't resist his military way."
        To a " right shoulder shift," etc.

Where'ere I go I greatly am admired,
And with such martial feeling I'm inspired,
That the ladies all assert that with me they'd rather flirt,
For of military men they're never tired.
        To a " right shoulder shift," etc.

THE FLANNEL MOUTH MICK.

Written by WILLIAM WELCH of Simmons and Slocum's Minstrels.

I KNOW you'll have pity
 When you hear what I say—
The way I have been treated
 By the blackguards each day,
Who stand on the corners,
 As I pass them by,
You can hear them say plainly,
 Arrah, "stag the old guy."

CHORUS.

Oh, they yell out, " You terrier,
 Go shoot that bat quick ! "
They call me a chow and
 A flannel mouth mick.

The other day while a-walking
 I went down the street,
A charming young damsel
 By chance I did meet ;
Says I, " You look charming,
 Ah, cushla ma vick ;"
Says she, " Drop on yourself,
 You flannel mouth mick."
      Oh, they yell out, etc.

When election day comes,
 I know what they'll say—
" How are you, Mr. McGuinness,
 How are you ? good day. "
They'll hand me a ticket,
 Say, " Go vote it, now quick—"
I'm a gentleman then,
 And no flannel mouth mick.
      Oh, they yell out, etc.

KALAMAZACK.

She's gone to join the circus,
  She's an actor in the ring,
She's teaching the elephant how to dance,
  And the hip-po-po-tamus to sing;
I know I'll never see her more,
  She's travelling now by rail,
She's getting ten dollars a day, my boys,
  For scrubbing the monkey's tail.

CHORUS.

  For she is my morning glory,
    And I wish she would come back;
  I'd buy her a bran new pair of socks,
    Likewise a summer straw hat,
  A pound of cheese, a barrel of fleas;
    I'd ride her out in a hack,
  My beautiful, sweet Elizabeth,
    From the town of Kalamazack.

When first we was acquainted
  She was with the soap-fat man,
She was chewing glue for Miss Barue,
  Who keeps a peanut stand;
But now she's getting wealthy,
  She has left me here forlorn;
I hope she'll die or get rammed in the eye,
  With a rack-o-ri-nuses' horn.

                    For she is, etc.

I can't live any longer
  Unless she does return;
I'll swallow a stool or a three-legged mule,
  Or I'll cut off my head with a churn.
And if that doesn't kill me,
  Myself I'll tie in a sack—
I'll jump in the river and take a bath,
  For my Lizzie of Kalamazack.

                    For she is, etc.

ALDERMAN FLYNN.

Written by GEORGE THATCHER, the great Ethiopian Comedian.

I GUESS you have heard of fighting, (*Symp.*)
Now, that's what I delight in ; (*Symp.*)
As I go down the street, boys,
　With my sword drawn in my hand,
I march to the tune of the Mulligan Guards,
　As played by the Irish band.

CHORUS.

There's Alderman Flynn, what do you think of him ?
He is elected now by a thousand solid men ;
And the boys all shout when I turn out,
Hurrah, for Alderman Flynn !

I am pet, of all the ladies, (*Symp.*)
I am fond of all the babies ; (*Symp.*)
My appearance is engaging—
It is upon my word.
I expect to be a solid man
Over all the wards.
　　　　　.　There's Alderman Flynn, etc.

I thought I'd go to the army, (*Symp.*)
I thought the bullets wouldn't harm me ; (*Symp.*)
I went to go to the rear one day, for to get cup of tea,
When a cannon ball come,
And hit me in the thumb,
And knocked the leg off me.

SPOKEN.—When I came home a wounded hero it was different. They wanted me to grind an organ on the corners ; they
said one good turn deserves another, and now the boys say
when they see me—

CHORUS.

Alderman Flynn, with his dizzy shin,
That hat he wears has been called in ;
And they all do shout when I turn out,
There's dizzy Alderman Flynn.

THE LABORING MAN.

Written by GEORGE THATCHER.

MY name it is Pat Connors,
  I am happy as you can see;
I was born in Cork in Ireland,
  That emerald of the sea ;
I left my native country,
  My dear old native sod,
And earned an honest living here
  By carrying the hod.

CHORUS.

  So gaze upon me, while I'm here,
    I will do the best I can,—
  My motives are pure, although I am poor,
    And only a laboring man.

When I came to this country
  A dollar a day was good,
But now if a man gets two and half
  It will scarcely buy him food ;
But I will struggle through the world,
  And do the best I can—
I'll stick to politics, and some day
  I'll be an alderman.
                         So gaze, etc.

Oh, when the war it broke out,
  I for a soldier did go,
I shouldered my gun in the 69th,
  And you know we were not slow ;
It was down upon Virginia's soil,
  With General Kearney we gave them the gripes,
For all true-born Irishmen
  Stick up for the stars and stripes.
                         So gaze, etc.

MRS. CASEY'S RAFFLE.

Written and sung by HARRY KERNELL.

If you listen to me for awhile
   I'll tell you a tale;
You all know Mrs. Casey, down
   The street, that sells the ale.
She gave a raffle for a stove,
   And to have a dance as well;
And·I being the floor manager,
   Had tickets for to sell.

SPOKEN.—Mrs. Casey is a particular friend of John McSwegan, and a full cousin of William Waterhouse; and her husband Sam O'Casey, *alias* Gas House Sam—(he was once employed in the Gas House at sixty dollars a month, wheeling smoke out in a push-cart)—he went to the war as a soldier, and never returned, and Mrs. Casey raffled off the old stove.

CHORUS.

But oh, what a row! I will tell it to you now!
Breaking heads, with slats of the beds;
McGuffin fainted, I thought he was dead,
O'Brien lost his hat, what do you think of that?
Mrs. O'Leary lost her hoops at Casey's raffle!

Now, in came John McIntee,
   Along with Rodger Dunbar;
When up jumped O'Brien, the fiddler,
   And says, this is going too far.
But before he had time to open his mouth,
   He was lying on the floor;
And I like a fighting man,
   Busted through the door.

SPOKEN.—Begorra, I never saw such a fracas in my born days before. Whin they knocked O'Brien down, he bawled out for Nixey, and cheese it; and they came in with billy-jacks, and knocked every body down that came in reach of them. And Nancy McGowan got excited and jumped clear out of a pull-back dress.

But oh! what a row, etc.

The raffling then did commence,
   As you may understand;
McGuffin threw forty-four,
   And O'Donnell called his hand.
But, Mrs. Casey got vexed then,
   And ordered thim all out;
When the fiddler played Patrick's day,
   Then you had ought to hear them shout.

(1)

MRS. CASEY'S RAFFLE.—Concluded.

SPOKEN.—Such shouting you never heard in your life; but when the supper was announced, everything became quiet. They had a splendid supper. There was mackerel and ice-cream, and molasses and oysters. John Bradley went to wait on the ladies. He asked one girl what she would have ? Says she, "I will have quail." Says John, "You will have bean soup, or you will give your seat to Biddy Doyle." Another young girl wanted an egg dropped on toast; says John, "You will get some old hen to drop it, or you will not get it here to-night." Then Bermidas Conklin wanted to make a speech. Says he, "Would I were an eagle, that I might fly over the sea and spread the liberty of my country !" Says Jim Kelly, "Sit down; you would be shot for a goose before you got half way." But it was—

But oh! what a row, etc.

THERE'S A BOTTLE ON THE MANTLE.

AIR.—"Letter in the Candle."

THERE's a bottle on the mantle,
  But it don't belong to me ;
If I could only smell the flavor,
  How happy I would be.
But I dare not approach it,
  For fear some one would come in ;
But I would like to take a snifter,
  For I know it's full of gin.

CHORUS.

Small drop of gin,
  To wet my fiery tongue ;
I loved you since my childhood,
  Many songs of you I have sung.

Oh! how sadly I remember,
  It was two short months ago ;
I had a bully lunch route,
  But they took me down below.
They said I was a vagarant—
  And I think it was a sin
To lock me in a dungeon,
  And deprive me of my gin.
        Small drop of gin, etc.

(2)

THE SCAMP;

OR, THEY CAN'T HOLD A CANDLE TO ME.

Written by HENRY PETTITT.   *Composed by* LANCE MAJOR.

I flat - ter my - self I'm a rogue.... And

can - did - ly own I'm a cad.... A sharp, a

leg, a va - ga-bond, And ev - ry thing else that is

bad. I proved to my pa - rents a bane, A

per - fect young fiend to my nurse; And ev - e - ry

year I con - tin - ue to live, I'm get - ting from

Chorus.

bad to worse. Oh! if there was ev er a

scamp, I flat - ter my-self I am he; From

(1)

THE SCAMP.—[Concluded.]

William   the   Norman   to   Brigham   the Mormon,   They

can't   hold   a   can - dle   to   me.

I was leader in mischief at school,
   Though always so humble and meek ;
And when I discovered a chance of reward,
   I was always informer and sneak.
By the evil example I set,
   Other boys into mischief were led ;
But I always managed to pocket the spoil,
   And get other boys wolloped instead.—Cmo.

When a man I went into the world,
   I plundered the helpless and poor ;
Yet always got off with a snug little sum,
   When it came to a question of law.
I started benevolent funds,
   And spouted at Exeter Hall,
I started loan offices, hospitals, clubs,
   And finally swindled them all.—Cho.

In the City my name I keep up,
   And swindling comp'nies promote ;
Yet always creep out with the bulk of the funds,
   Before it's found out it won't float.
I'm an alderman, and as M. P.
   To stand I've received an invite ;
And if I get in, why, my party I'll sell,
   And Gladstone will make me a knight.—Cho.

(2)

PAY FOR THE LAST ROUND.

AIR.—"Wait till the Moonlight."

Down in the Fourth Ward on a pleasant little corner,
I compliment myself I own a liquor store ;
It is not a place like where Jack Horner
Eat his Christmas pudding, but a far superior place.
It is not a cafe—it is not a palace,
It is not a dew drop inn, or any such a place ;
We are not at all gallus—we do not take taffy,
But always look a man square in the face.

SPOKEN.—Yes, I have a fine saloon now. But I have a great
time with the young fellows that frequent my saloon. A man
came in the other day and asked for a kerosene cock-tail.
Says I, "Maybe you want a coal-oil lamp punch ?" Says he,
"I'll punch you, if you come out from behind the bar." Says
I, "Me young stripling, if I walk around there and hit you with
my left hand, I will fell you like an ox." Says he back then
to me, "You have too much chin for a terrier ;" and says I,
"You have too much lip for a bull pup." But he sat down and
called for a glass of porter. He didn't pay for it, and when he
called for another, says I—

CHORUS.

Pay for the last round, that's what you called for,
Then you can have anything you want ;
But until you do, sir, the next one you call for,
I will bet you five dollars you'll get the bounce.

My wife was a German before we were married,
Her name it was Katrina, or something of the kind ;
We live about as quiet—we never do get flurried,
She's a thoroughbred you can bet your life, and I am glad
she's mine.
She is not a dandy, or a cologne water daisy,
She's very neat and hardy is my mistress Jane O'Doyle ;
We are a couple to admire, if you knew her you would say,
We don't set the world on fire, but always pay our way.

SPOKEN.—Last week I took in some boarders, and I have had
no peace since. One was a circus actor, and he took the feather bed in the cellar, and be heavens he commenced practising
pyramids on it. The other was a Negro actor, and done nothing but yah yah here, and yah yah there. When I asked him
his name, says he, "I am Cully, the cutter!" and I hear since

(1)

PAY FOR THE LAST ROUND.—Concluded.

it is Jimmy Rodgers. Divil the cent of board have they paid
since they came. The other morning I told them not to be so
familiar with the butter, that there was good molasses on the
table. Says they, " Oh, shoot the molasses !" Says I, "Don't do
that ;" and when the meat is put on the table, they make a glam
at the lean and leave the fat for the other boarders. But I will
get rid of the boarders as quick as I can, and start a lunch
bar. I asked my wife the other day if she liked oysters? She
said " The only oyster she ever ate was a clam, and it made her
sick." But you can bet any man comes in my saloon only
cheats me once, for I say—

Pay for the last round, etc.

IRISH BLADES.

Sung by MURPHY and MORTON.

WE'RE two roving blades from old Killarney,
And the pretty colleens call us bouncing Barneys ;
We're the Irish boys can tip to them the blarney,
And dear old Paddy's Land, that's our home, do you mind ;
Just a few years ago we took a notion
For to take a trip across the briny ocean ;
Our hearts were all in a commotion,
Since we left that little isle so far away, do you mind.

CHORUS.

For we are ever bright and gay, singing, dancing all the day,
This caubeen of a hat we're ever wearing,
Although we are from our homes afar,
Our hearts are ever there ;
No land we'll ever see can ever wean
Our love from dear old Ireland.

When we landed in Columbia's nation,
Among the girls we caused a great sensation ;
We're the happiest Irish pair that's in the nation,
And dear old Paddy's land that's our home, do you mind ;
When at night the bright eyes are glancing,
For the colleens fair you will always see us dancing,
We are two Irish boys that's always fond of prancing,
And to please you sure that is our aim.

For we are, etc.

(2)

PARADE OF THE A. O. H.

Written for HARRY KERNELL by G. A. McCURDY.

AIR—" Connemara Coockoos."

I'm a gay young chap from Erin and they call me Dandy Pat,
I wear a green regalia, a harp, and shamrock in my hat;
I joined the Ancient Order; we're the boys that looked so gay
When we marched in the procession on last St. Patrick's day,
And oh, such music, such music, such music as we had all day,
Such music, such music, how sweet the bands did play.

Hugh Maginnis was chief marshal and he rode a fine white horse,
With a sword and sash beside him, oh! boys he was the boss!
With a smile on every feature, and a uniform so gay,
The ladies all smiled on him as we marched along the way,
And oh, such winking, such winking, such winking as was
  there that day,
Such winking, such winking, they winked the livelong day.

'Twas just below the common we fell into the line,
With flags and banners flying, the day being nice and fine,
The band played Garry Owen and then the Mulligan Guard;
And we carried the harp of Erin beside the stripes and stars.
And oh, such tramping, such tramping, such tramping as was
  there that day,
Such tramping, such tramping all through the mud and clay.

When we marched in open order faith 'twould make you laugh
  to see
The little stick leg cripple keeping step with Mick Magee;
When we come before the marshal's house they brought us to
  a halt,
And they gave us just ten minutes for to go and get our malt.
And oh, such whiskey, such whiskey, such whiskey as was
  drank that day,
Such whiskey, such whiskey, the bar-rooms made it pay.

Then when we were disbanded as quick as you could wink
We all bounced down to Kelley's for to have a drop to drink,
The whiskey punch flew lively for the liquor was so rare,
In less than fifteen minutes divil a sober man was there.
And oh, such drinking, such drinking, such drinking as was
  there that night,
Such drinking, such drinking, the boys got awful tight.

Mike Connors and Pat Cronin then got into a dispute,
Mike said his hat was finest, and Pat slapped him on the snoot,
Then broken heads were plenty, the blood ran freely there,
Myself and long Dan Carty had to waltz off on our ear.
And oh, such fighting, such fighting, such fighting as the boys
  had there,
Such fighting, such fighting, 'twas like an Irish fair.

JUST LIKE JOHN.

Sung by MATT WHEELER.

DEY held a camp meeting down in de swamp,
    Going to Jerusalem just like John!
It was so dark dey had to have a lamp,
    Going to Jerusalem just like John!
De preacher preached long, den he preach loud,
    Going to Jerusalem just like John!
He preached so bad he scared de whole crowd,
    Going to Jerusalem just like John!

CHORUS.

When I die I want to be ready,
When I die I want to be ready,
When I die I want to be ready
Going to Jerusalem just like John!

Oh, sisters, what make you so cranky?
    Going to Jerusalem just like John!
You got as much chance as Moody and Sankey,
    Going to Jerusalem just like John!
When de horn blows we'll be dar,
    Going to Jerusalem just like John!
To climb upon de golden stair,
    Going to Jerusalem just like John!
             When I die, etc.

THE FUNNY LITTLE TAILOR.

Composed and sung by PAT KELLY.

THERE was a jolly tailor once that I knew well,
He kept a little tailor shop and had pantaloons to sell,
Neck-ties, broadcloth, and everything like that,
And anyone could tell he wore a very funny hat;
It wasn't very low nor it wasn't very high,
It had a peculiar look that would quickly take the eye.
He wore it on Sunday and every day in the week,
And it always looked glossy, for he kept it very neat.

He was the pride of the ladies and the envy of the boys;
Wherever he would go he would never make a noise;
He was as light on his feet as a canary on a tree;
He was bashful, he was neat, and as happy as could be;
Whenever there was a party he was sure to be there,
With his tight pantaloons and glossy curly hair;
He could talk, dance, sing, and wink, and everything like that,
But no matter where he would go he wore his funny little hat.

He went to a party one night where there was lots of fun,
He got rather tired and sleepy from drinking rum and gum!
They put him in the corner to have a little doze,
When the boys found it out they put a cork on his nose,
And they all yelled " Fire !" with a terrible shout;
But he quickly jumped up and quietly put it out;
He took his little hat and walked to the door,
And he bade them all good-bye, and they never saw him more.

JUST LANDED.

AIR.—"I Couldn't Stay Away."

WE came from Connemara
  A few short months ago,
With spirits light and airy,
  Two emigrants, you know;
Pray let us ask your pardon,
  Smile on us if you choose,
We come to Castle Garden,
  We're the two Irish cuckoos.

CHORUS.

For we've just landed, just landed,
  We landed over there, you know;
We've landed, just landed,
  We're the two Irish cuckoos.

Cutting turf was our occupation
  In the bogs of Allen then;
But they say that in this nation
  We'll at least be aldermen; .
We'll run for big positions
  In offices of note,
We'll join the politicians,
  And of course for us you'll vote.
          For we've just, etc.

When we go back to Ireland,
  Sure, then it will be said
We'll raise up in our sire-land
  The green above the red;
Then all this world will glory
  Whene'er they hear the news
Of Ireland and the story of
  The two Irish cuckoos.
          For we've just, etc.

THE RISING POLITICIAN.

Written and sung by HARRY BENNETT.

GOOD evening to ye all,
I've come to make a call,
And tell ye of my victory
   Upon election day.
I ran for alderman,
And Murphy was the man
Who tried hard to defeat me,
   But he gave himself away;
He never tried repeatin',
And that's the way I beat him—
I voted seven times myself
   In the ould Fourth Ward so gay.
     CHORUS.
    Now I'm a politician,
    I hold a high position
    I gained by repetition
    Upon election day.

I took the gang around
Where the free lunch could be found,
And many's the plate of soup, my boys,
   Did they put out of sight;
We swept the district clean,
And the divil such a scene
Was known in New York city, boys,
   Upon election night;
Cigar signs, barrels, boards we burned
When the victory it was earned
It gave me satisfaction and
   It filled me wid delight.
     Now I'm a politician, etc.

And now I'll tell to you
What I am going to do;
I'll not forget the workingmen,
   To them I will be true;
They shall have eight hours a day,
And a fair amount of pay,
And live as well as those big bugs
   Upon Fifth Avenue;
Sure I'll improve the city,
For I think it is a pity
That poor men should be starving
   When there's public work to do.
     CHORUS.
    So let ye all be merry,
    And don't ye vote contrary,
    And I will show ye, one and all,
    What an Irishman can do.

DUBLIN POLICEMEN.

We're rattling, roaring Irish boys,
    Come over here to join the force, man;
To protect the peace, keep down the noise,
    There's none can do it like us, of course, man;
In our suit of blue there are but few
    With us can come the Irish dandy,
And if the boys kick up any noise,
    Sure we run them into the cell quite handy.

CHORUS.

Tearing away, (*Symp.*)
Always at war and never at peace, man,
    Tue ral a loo, (*Symp.*)
We're a pair of the Dublin new policemen.

There's not a gate nor garden wall
    About the town but what we scale it,
And if anything there we find at all,
    Wouldn't we be flats if we didn't nail it?
Next day there is a hue and cry,
    Something stole, but to be brief, man,
And by the hookey, who but ourselves
    Is running about to cotch the thief, man!
                            Tearing away, etc.

Supposing, walking about all night,
    In every hole and corner creeping,
Something we spy by the pale moonlight;
    Arrah, by my soul, it's a gintleman sleeping,
His pockets we grope, his money we take,
    Then with our sticks on the ribs we're jobbing him,
And if perchance the poor soul should wake,
    We tell him we thought a thief was robbing him.
                            Tearing away, etc.

A TWO-CENT SAIL.

Written and sung by HARRY BENNETT.

THE other night, while feeling bright,
    I thought I'd have a racket ;
The thought itself was good enough,
    But I'd no stamps to back it.
I went to take a two-cent sail,
    To keep my spirits merry,
But now I wish that I had died
    Before I crossed the ferry.

CHORUS.

    With lively boys and witching girls,
        I tell you it was merry ;
    I never shall forget that night
        A-crossing on the ferry.

I paid my fare and jumped aboard—
    The weather it was breezy ;
I didn't care for wind or rain,
    For I am free and easy ;
And I began to think and think
    About Beecher and Frank Moulton,
When all at once I felt a bunk,
    And then a fearful jolting.
                With lively boys, etc.

I felt a crash, and up I jumped,
    There was a fearful clatter ;
I looked about, and then went out
    To see what was the matter.
A gal was yelling murder, and
    She was a fearful screecher—
I saw a man fall overboard,
    She said that it was Beecher.
                With lively boys, etc.

Then overboard I quickly jumped
    To try and save the preacher,
Because I thought it would be great
    To rescue Henry Beecher ;
But when I struck the water, oh !
    You bet it set me screaming ;
I found that I had been asleep,
    And jumped overboard while dreaming.
                With lively boys, etc.

THE SELDOM-FED BRIGADE.

Words and Music by HARRY BENNETT.

WE are the Seldom-Fed Brigade,
    As you can plainly see ;
We often have to miss our meals—
    With us it don't agree.
One meal a day is all we get,
    For that we have to fight,
Oatmeal for breakfast, wind for lunch,
    And a walk around at night.

CHORUS.

We're the Seldom-Fed Brigade,
    For fighting we're not paid,
And for our grub we get a club—
    That's how our soup is made ;
If soon we are not paid,
    We'll have to make a raid,
To drive away starvation from
    The Seldom-Fed Brigade.

If we could strike a hash mill or
    A lunch route on the street,
You bet our baskets we would fill,
    We'd show you how to eat ;
We'd pulverize a restaurant,
    Or clean out a hotel ;
If we can't get a square meal, why,
    Just let us take a smell.
                        We're the, etc.

Wind pudding's all we get to eat,
    Of that we're awful sick,
And if we ask for other grub,
    They'll hit us with a brick ;
We'll soon be healthy skeletons—
    Our clothes are getting loose ;
Oh, if you want to see us bust,
    Just chuck us down a goose.
                        We're the, etc.

"UP A TREE."

By HARRY CLIFTON.

You see be-fore you one who's been in life through ma-ny a chang-ing scene, And yet with-al a lit-tle green, of course, I know it now: Although I've been un-for-tu-nate, you will al-low me to re-late That once I owned a large es-tate—'twas then friends used to bow; "Dear Jack, old boy," they then would say, "I'm proud of such a meet-ing! How do you do? Where have you been! You're look-ing well, I see;" But now they've grown so very shy they can't af-ford a greet-ing; In vul-gar phra-se-ol-o-gy, be-cause I'm "up a tree."

(1)

"UP A TREE."—[CONCLUDED.]

Chorus.

I'd friends in great va - ri - e - ty, who courted my so - ci - e - ty;

Came to dine, drank my wine, shook my hand with glee—I might

walk from now till whitsuntide, but when they see me, off they glide And

pass me on the oth - er side, be - cause I'm "up a tree."

I once could give good dinners, ah, 'twas then the hungry sinners
Would haunt my table daily, praise my judgment, jokes and wine;
Join in conviviality, accept my hospitality,
Until, through prodigality, my fortune did decline.
And so did they, for one by one they left me in my glory,
A friend I stood in need of, but not one could I see;
My money'd gone and so had they; well, 'tis the same old story,
So while you have it, keep it, or you'll soon be "up a tree."
    Chorus :—I'd friends, &c.

I once could drive my four-in-hand, had money, too, at my command,
Could " do the grand," you understand—how foolish I have been!
I stand here to exemplify " sweet uses of adversity,"
To prove my friends in poverty—acquaintances, I mean:
Better times will come again, a lesson 'twill have taught me—
" Preserve me from my friends," for the future it shall be;
I've paid for my experience, tho' you see to what it's brought me,
I'm a " sadder, yet a wiser man," although I'm " up a tree."
    Chorus :—I'd friends, &c.

(2)

THE SLIGO MUSKETEERS.

Words and Music by HARRY BENNETT.

Oh, let ye stand from under now and open wide your ears,
While we relate the story of the Sligo Musketeers ;
Sure, whin we landed on this soil out West they made us go,
And we worked at canaling on the Oh—ho—ho ;
But whin the war it did break out it took our job away,
We organized a company and wint into the fray ;
We fought the ragged rebels, boys, for many a weary day,
But they couldn't bate the Sligo Musketeers.

CHORUS.

With our ha, ha, ha, ha, hay foot straw, we marched across
    the plain,
And many's the time we thought we'd never see our homes
    again ;
The rebels fought like divils, but their fighting was in vain,
For they couldn't bate the Sligo Musketeers.

We fought wid Banks and Burnside, and wid Grant we took a
    hack,
But the best of all, tho' he was small, was gallant little Mac ;
Faith, if they'd let him have his way, he'd quickly drive them
    back,
    If assisted by the Sligo Musketeers ;
Sure he knew how to engineer and likewise to command—
No matter what your station was he'd take you by the hand ;
He looked so noble on his horse when he was in command
    Of us fighting boys, the Sligo Musketeers.
                                With our ha, ha, etc.

But now our lave of absence, boys, is very nearly spint,
We'd ax ye all to have a smile, but we're without a cint ;
On Erie shares and all such snares our money it is lent—
    It completely broke the Sligo Musketeers ;
We'll say, "Good evening, one and all," your pardon, too, we
    crave ;
We did our duty manfully this country for to save ;
May the shamrock and the stars and stripes in triumph ever
    wave
    O'er the fortunes of the Sligo Musketeers.
                                With our ha, ha, etc.

BEAUTIFUL BOY.

Air—" Darling Ould Stick.

It was one winter's day, about six in the morn,
When a little innocent creature was born;
There was doctor and nurse, and a great many more,
But none of them saw such a baby before.
   They all swore I was like my papa,
   " Yes, and see, there's the nose of his mamma
   With a few alterations, oh, la, la,
. We'll make him a beautiful boy."

" To make him a beauty," cried out Mrs. Sneer,
" We'll be troubled unless the child has a sweet leer."
Then to give me this leer Mrs. Glazier arose,
And a piece of red putty stuck bang on my nose.
   This made me to wink and to blink so,
   The ladies knew not what to think, oh,
   And at last it turned into a squint, oh,
    Which made me a beautiful boy.

To make me accomplished, I wanted one thing,
My mouth was too small for the dear child to sing,
Then to stretch it and spread it they all of them tried,
Till they stretched my sweet mouth nearly half a yard wide
   Crying: " Pull away now, Mrs. Rider,
   It must be a little bit wider."
   My dear mouth they split pretty high, sir,
    All to make me a beautiful boy,

Now, being complete, I was next sent to school,
And to show off my make, was stuck on a high stool,
When the children went home, they cried out with surprise:
" We have a new boy at school with such beautiful eyes!
   He can look any way so handy,
   Such a mouth he has got to suck candy !
   And his legs are so preciously bandy,
    They call him the beautiful boy."

T'other day I was asked in the city to dine,
The ladies. in raptures, all thought me divine;
And all, when observing my elegant grace,
Neglected their dinner to look at my face.
   They cried: " I shall faint with surprise !
   No gas-lights can equal his eyes,
   And such a mouth for mince-pies !
    Law! ain't he a beautiful boy !"

Now, ladies, beware of Love's powerful darts,
For fearful I am I shall steal all your hearts,
And then, you dear, sweet little creatures, you'll sigh,
And doat on my charms till you languish and die.
   For, you know, I can't marry you all,
   Yet, believe me, whenever you call,
   My endeavors will be to please all,
    Although such a beautiful boy.

A TERRIBLE EXAMPLE.

Words and Music by Joseph P. Skelly.

The Music of this song is published by E. H. Harding, 229 Bowery, New York. Price 10 cents.

McGee was a jolly old cobbler,
  He came from the divil knows where ;
Of whiskey, he was a great gobbler,
  And delighted to go on a " tare."
He was often persuaded to alter
  His habits, and live like a man ;
But whenever he tried, he would falter,
  And go back to his bottle and can.

CHORUS.

McGee was a terrible man,
  He was always so flighty and frisky ;
He tried to reform, but he couldn't keep warm,
  Sure, he'd die if he hadn't his whiskey.

His wife was a dacent ould woman,
  And scolded from mornin' till night ;
She told him he must be inhuman
  To be keeping them in such a plight.
He would listen in scorn and derision,
  And drink just as much as before ;
Till at length she gave out her decision
  To begin on a temperance war.
                          McGee was, etc.

She went to a temperance preacher
  And stated the case of McGee ;
He promised to help the poor creature—
  " I'll go over next mornin'," says he.
When he came, the old cobbler was roaring
  A song, with his glass in his hand ;
'Twas the glass he was fond of adoring,
  And he seemed hardly able to stand !
                          McGee was, etc.

" Dear Misther McGee," said his rev'rence,
  " I hope you will alter your ways ;
I've come now to give you deliverance
  From the evil that's blighting your days !"
" 'Pon me sowl !" says McGee, " I am ready,
  I'll stop with the greatest of cheer ;
But I fear I can never be steady
  While a dhrop of good whiskey is near."
                          McGee was, etc.

(1)

A TERRIBLE EXAMPLE.—Concluded.

"Fear not," said the man of cold water,
  "You'll show us how good you can be ;
The demon of drink we will slaughter,
  And we'll honor the name of McGee."
Then he promised to keep at a distance
  All drinks of whatever degree ;
"Noble man, you shall have our assistance—
  In a week the result we will see."
                McGee was, etc.

SPOKEN.—The reverend gentleman, after some further per-
suasions, took his departure, and Mr. McGee at once became a
strict disciple of temperance. The sudden change of life had a
severe effect upon him ; he lost all his exuberant spirits, being entirely under the control of his wife and the temperance
advocates, who filled his mind every day with solemn lectures,
and worked him into such a queer state—half comfort, half de-
spair—that he would often say to himself, "Begob, I'm not
meself at all !" At last they induced him to state in a public
meeting the various benefits he had derived from his adherence
to the pledge—the comfort, the happiness, the great joy and
peace of mind he had experienced during his short season of
sobriety He attended the meeting, and with a very grave
countenance, related his experience as follows :

RECITATION.

Good people, I stand here before you to-night,
Me mouth very dhry, and me head very light ;
It's three weeks to-day since I joined in the ranks
Of the Wather Brigade, I left off me ould pranks !
And ever since then, sure, me life has been blessed
With a great many comforts, and nights of good rest.
I paid all me debts, and I bought a new gown
For the wife of me bosom—a beautiful brown—
I took from the pawn shop me foin Sunday coat,
Which cost me last winter a ten dollar note,
And put a new sole on the ould woman's shoes—
A moighty big job, for she wears "twinty-two's !"
I made a new sty for the fine little pigs,
And fixed up the garden with bushes and twigs ;
I wint to a lawyer and made out my will,
My duty to all I was bound to fulfill.
And yesterday mornin' (don't think that I'm scoffin'),
I bought for me body an illigant coffin !
For I know if my whiskey is taken from me,
You'll very soon make a dead man of McGee.
                McGee was, etc.

BOSTON BEANS.

As sung by Ed. French Sheridan, Mack & Day's Grand Combination.

Air.—"Spring, Gentle Spring."

Beans, beans, Boston baked beans,
Served up red-hot on a Sunday morn ;
Beans, beans, Boston baked beans,
Is a fit dish for a queen, sure as you're born ;
Whenever you come to Boston town,
Have some one to show you round ;
Smoking red-hot upon the plates—
Yes, how I love those Yankee dates ;
You may talk about your good clam chowder,
Talk about your whiskey sour—

CHORUS.

Give me beans, beans, Boston baked beans,
Served up red-hot on a Sunday morn ;
Coffee, sugar, bread, and cream—
It's a fit dish for a queen, sure as you're born.

Cheese, cheese, Limburger cheese,
Floating so gayly and sweet in the breeze ;
Cheese, cheese, Limburger cheese—
Bring me a dish of sweet Limburger cheese ;
At Miller's saloon I take my ease,
And revel on lager and Limburger cheese ;
There is good, and for all of that,
For it gives you such a sweet breath ;
Talk of love in Cupid's hours—
Talk of a balm of a thousand flowers—

CHORUS.

Cheese, cheese, Limburger cheese,
Floating so gayly and sweet in the breeze ;
Cheese, cheese, Limburger cheese—
Bring me a dish of sweet Limburger cheese.

THE BARD OF ARMAGH.

As sung by NED HARRIGAN.

O ! list to the lay of a poor Irish harper,
  And scorn not the strains of his old withered hands,
But, remember those fingers, they once could move sharper,
  In raising the merry strains to his dear native land,
It was long before the shamrock, dear isle, lovely emblem,
  Was crushed in its beauty, by the Saxon's lion paw,
And all the pretty colleens around me would gather
  Call me their bold Phelim Brady, the Bard of Armagh.

How I love to muse on the days of my boyhood,
  Though four score and three years have flew by them,
It's king's sweet reflection that every young joy,
  For the merry-hearted boys make the best of old men.
At a fair, or a wake I could twist my shillelah,
  And trip through a dance wid my brogues tied with straw,
There all the pretty maidens around me would gather,
  Call me their bold Phelim Brady, the Bard of Armagh.

In truth I have wandered this wide world all over,
  Yet Ireland's my home and a dwelling for me,
And oh, let the turf that my old bones shall cover,
  Be cut from the land that is trod by the free ;
And when serjeant death in his cold arms doth embrace,
  And lull me to sleep with old Erin-go-bragh,
By the side of my Kathleen, my dear pride, oh place me,
  Then forget Phelim Brady, the Bard of Armagh.

THE BROTH OF A BOY IS PADDY.

Written and arranged by BILLY ASHCROFT.

AIR.—"The Boys of Kilkenny."

Oн, there's not in ould Ireland a boy half so free .
  As bould Paddy Flynn—be me sowl, and that's me ;
At breaking the hearts of the girls I am A 1,
  And at breaking the heads of the boys, beat by none
At breaking the skulls of the boys, banged by none.

"AIR.—Sally, come up,"

At making love, sir, Pat's the boy ;
  The ladies' hearts can't I decoy ?
Sure don't they gambol, kiss, and toy,
  And galivant with Paddy ;
And then so shy I wink my eye,
  Awhile the darlint creatures, ay.

AIR.—"Be aisy, can't you, Paddy !"

Paddy can stuff the blarney down,
  Paddy can grief in whiskey drown,
And crack a bottle, joke, or crown,
  Such a broth of a boy is Paddy.

AIR.—"Lowback Car."

Last night I went a courting,
  And met with a mishap ;
At Judy Riley's windy
  I went to give a rap :
But bad luck to the cistern
  Poor Paddy stood upon,

(1)

'Twas like the tricks of politics—
Not to be depended on,
For no sooner had I put
The sowl of me iligant foot
On the lid, than it slipped,
And whish !—in I was dipped
Souse head over heels in the butt.

Air.—"St. Patrick's Day."

Faith, so many I've admired, I'm getting tired
Of courting the smart little lasses at all ;
I've tipped 'em the blarney, but spite of me blarney
They've bid Paddy (bad luck !) good morning !
I've kilt all my rivals again and again,
And nine times for love it's meself that's been slain !
Wid grief I am laden, for fear an ould maiden
I'll die without wedlock adorning.

Air.—" The Ould Bog Hole."

So now, who'll marry a nate Irishman ?
For a lady I'll do all iver I can ;
I'm not very rich, but I'm born to good luck,
I've a cow just died and a dropsical duck ;
I'm expecting a fortune, and sure it won't fail
To come—when the income tax they repale.
Shall I spake to the praist to make it all right,
And order for music a *piany fortnight ?*
Who'll wed a boy from the Emerald Isle ?
Who'll on the suit of a bold Paddy smile ?
Who'll send a letter me grief to beguile ?
To Pat Number One-ty-one Lower Turnstile.

Who'll wed a boy, etc.

(2)

AN ILIGANT WAKE.

AIR.—" Darling Ould Stick."

Sung by BILLY ASHCROFT.

In Dublin, that city of riches and fame,
A shoemaker died, Jerry Flynn was his name,
The neighbors all grieved, rich and poor, high and low,
And to the wake of poor Jerry resolved for to go.

SPOKEN.—Poor Jerry! Though he often *half*-soled shoes, he
was a *whole*-souled man himself, and many's the job he done for
nothing. He mended Tim Reilly's brogans, and pegged Mrs.
M'Carthy, and gave her a new patch on her upper, an' all for
sixpence; so no wondher they all came to his wake. Tim
Donohoe wint for a coach for the ladies; he stuffed the fine soft
straw feather bed in the bottom of Con Casey's wheelbarrow;
he smoothed down the long feathers for fear any of them might
stick in the ladies, and hurt their—feelings, as he handed them
in.

CHORUS.

Mrs. Casey and Mrs. O'Blaney,
Kate Nolan and Widow Delaney,
And the iligant Judy M'Shaney,
To go to the beautiful wake.

All dressed out so neat in their best Sunday clothes,
Wid Doherty showing his jolly red nose,
And another big party about twenty score,
All met them a knocking at Jerry Flynn's door.

SPOKEN.—"Mrs. Flynn! Mrs. Flynn! why the blazes don't
you open the door? Here's the quality coming to Jerry's wake.
Stick him up slantindickler in the bed; clap a clane pipe in his
mouth and put a nightcap on him, that he may look nate and
dacint. Mistress Biddy, will you shake some clane straw in the
corner for the company to sit down on? There yees are all now
as snug as a bug in a rug. Come, now, Darby Reilly, while
Nelly's mixing the punch, will you just tip us a bit of a song?"
"Faix I will, mam; I'll give you a verse from the Opery of Go
to the Divil and shake yourself." "Silence! Pat Doyle, I'll run
a sod of turf in your gob if you don't hould your tongue. Darby
Reilly is going to sing; silence."

(*Sings in a drawling tone.*)

AIR.—" Raging Canawl."

Oh, once I never thought I'd be
In this dejected state,
A poor, forlorn effigy
Bound down by hardship's fate.

(1)

The birds that flutter on yon tree,
   With terror strike my heart;
Aich star I see alarums me—
   Oh, why did I des-art ?

SPOKEN.—"Oh, wow, ow! I can't bear to sing any more, it's too distressing for my delicate nerves. Missus M'Nulty, will ye thry a song, mam?" "Thoth I will, Darby. Here goes."
(*Mrs. M'Nulty sings.*)

Och ! one evening for dervarsion's sake
   As I walked out alone,
I heard a faymalo lady bright
   Making her piteous moan.
She wrung her bands and tore her hair,
   And to herself did cry,
Aarrah, Johnny dear, don't murther me,
   For if you do I'll die.

SPOKEN.—Here's Nelly wid the punch, now hand it round to

Mrs. M'Carthy and Mrs. O'Blaney,
Kate Nolan and Widow Delaney,
And the beautiful Judy M'Shaney,
   And all at the iligant wake.

Now the whiskey went round till they couldn't agree,
Who was of the best rank or the best family;
They from words came to blows, and their fists didn't spare,
And by handfuls they pulled out each other's hair.

SPOKEN.—Oh, ladies! ladies ! aren't you forshamed av yourselves, to behave like a set of jackasses ! Oh Judy, Judy ! Judy! Divil roast me but they've got Jerry in amongst them ; they'll bate the life out of the corpse. Here, catch hoult of his toe and pull him out of the scrimmage. Haul away, here. We've got him out. Oh, bad luck to me, but they've give him a black eye. The brutes! to murther a poor dead man that way! Oh, he'll never get over it ; give me the broomstick, till I bate them all out, every one of them not excepting

Mrs. Casey and Mrs. O'Blaney,
Kate Nolan and Widow Delaney,
And the red-headed Judy M'Shaney,
   And all at the iligant wake.

(2)

A VIRGIN ONLY 19 YEARS OLD.

By Harry Rickards.

As I was out walk-ing one

night near the Strand, I met a fair

dam-sel all hooped up so grand, She had

feath-ers and fi-ne-ry, *Sym.* and

jew-els and gold,.. And she said she

was a vir-gin— yes, a vir-gin,

on-ly nine-teen years old!

(1)

A VIRGIN, ONLY 19 YEARS OLD. [Concluded.]

Her fingers were taper'd, her neck like the swan,
Her nose was a turn-up, and her voice not too strong;
In three weeks we were married, and the wedding bells told
That I'd married a virgin—yes, a virgin, only 19 years old!

The wedding-party broke up, and we retired to rest,
But my hair stood right up when my bride she undress'd;
For a cartload of padding my young bride did unfold,
A thing rather peculiar, very peculiar, for 19 years old!

First, she took off her right foot, about a foot wide,
Then she unscrewed her left ear and laid it aside,
Then she pull'd out her right eye, on the carpet it roll'd;
Thinks I, here's a virgin—what a virgin, only 19 years old!

Next she unscrewed her right leg as far as the knee,
Then pull'd off her fingers, I counted just three;
Then on her left shoulder a large lump I did behold,
So I said, there's a virgin—yes, a virgin, only 19 years old!

When she wiped off her eyebrows I thought I should faint,
And scraped from her thin cheeks a cartload of paint;
When she pull'd off her black wig then her bald pate soon told
That she was an old virgin, an old virgin, more than 19 years old!

When she pull'd out her false teeth, I jumped up in terror,
For her nose and her chin very near stuck together,
From the chamber I stepp'd it, never more to behold
This virgin not nineteen,—no, not nineteen, but 99 years old!

Now, young men, take warning, e'er to church you go,
Be sure your wife's perfect from the top to the toe,
Or you'll pay for your folly, and like me be sold
By some patch'd-up old virgin, cruel old virgin,'bout 99 years old

(2)

50

DIGGING FOR GOULD.

Darby Kelly below in Killkenny did live,
A sketch of whose character I'm going to give;
He was thought by the people a green polished rogue,
He could wastle the whiskey, or wastle the old brogue;
All kinds of diseases with herbs he could cure,
He'd interpret your dreams to be certain and sure,
By the boys of the village he often was fool'd;
For aslape or awake, he was dreaming of gould.
                    Fol de dol, &c.

He had a fine open house, but the winders were broke,
The gables were down to let out the smoke;
Some beautiful pigs, through the wide world to range,
Though they were thin, they were thick with the mange,
He was so neglectful of domestic affairs,
The rats eat the bottoms all out of the chairs,
And the wife by the husband was so overruled,
When she asked him for coppers. he was talking of gould.
                    Fol de dol, &c.

The house thus neglected, sure nothing went right;
When a youth of the village came to him, one night,
A nice boy he was, his name was Dan Mac,
And ready to fly with the duds on his back;
All the clothes that he had wasn't enough
To make him a bolster to stick on a crutch,
And his juvenile days in a lime-kiln were schooled,
But he used to cod Darby about finding gould.
                    Fol de dol, &c.

Says Dan; Ere last night I had a beautiful dream;
Bit bad luck to the doubt! last night I'd the same;
And to-day, as I dozed, after slacking some lime,
I dreamt it again for the third and last time.
Och, murder! says Darby, come tell us your dream,
Same time his two eyes like rockets did gleam,
Says Dan: I dreamt at the castle Kilcool
I found a jar that was crammed full of gould.
                    Fol de dol, &c.

DIGGING FOR GOULD.—[concluded.]

Poor Darby a big mouth opened like a dead Haicke,
Saying: You'll be a hero, just like your name-sake;
You'll ride in your coach, you fortunate elf,
While I may be in one, going down to the hulks.
No matter, said Darby, we must emigrate,
So, come down at mid-night, and don't be too late;
Bring some boys whose courage won't easy be cooled,
And we'll dig till daylight to find all the gould.
Fol de dol, &c.

They arrived at the castle, at about one o'clock,
Where Dan dreamt he found all the gold in a crock,
They all set to work with picks, shovels and spades.
And a hole, that would swallow a house, soon was made,
Says Darby: Bad luck to the curse we must give.
Or we'll be beggars as long as we live !
Says Dan: My the devil on my back be stooled,
For, I have bursted my breeches in digging for gould !
Fol de dol, &c.

The prayers availed nothing, the crock was soon found,
Tim Rooney he lifted it over the ground ;
With joy Darby leaped on the back of Ned Fail,
Like a fish from the stream with a hook in his tail,
Says Darby: My wife won't abuse me to-night,
When I take home the shiners so yellow and bright !
I'll buy house and land about Killcool.
And we'll all bless the night we went digging for gould !
Fol de dol, &c·

The crock was then placed on Darby's own back,
To carry home and each man have his whack,
They arrived at the door with the gould to be sacked,
When Mac with a spade knocked the crock into smash
Poor Darby, near smothered, ran in with affright ;
His wife jumps up to get him a light:
When she heard Darby mourning, her passion was cooled,
She knew by the smell he was covered with gould !
Fol de dol, &c.

DEAR OULD SOD.

It was down in Queenstown harbor,
   The morning I set sail,
My mammy cried to me, " Oh, John ;
   Your heart will never fail ;
You're leaving poor old Ireland,"
   My mother said to me ;
" Arrah, don't forget the dear ould sod
   Across the deep blue sea."

The boys and girls all 'round me
   Did shed the parting tear ;
My hungry eyes were fastened on
   The form to me so dear ;
She waved her poor old withered hand,
   And cried out, " John machree,
Arrah, don't forget the dear ould sod
   When you cross the deep blue sea."

The very winds did sob and moan,
   As we put out to sea,
A sad farewell to Ireland, growing,
   Dim upon our lee ;
But through my brain kept ringing still
   Her parting words to me—
" Arrah, don't forget the dear ould sod
   When you cross the deep blue sea."

When I landed in New York
   I felt both strange and queer ;
'Twas soon I had the money earned
   To bring the old mother here,
And as she stepped upon the dock
   She cried, " Grah gra, machree,
You didn't forget the dear ould sod
   When you cross'd the deep blue sea."

The old dark days have passed and gone,
   Their grip no more we'll feel ;
There's bread for every man who'll put
   His shoulder to the wheel ;
But while we're living here beneath
   The banner of the free,
We'll ne'er forget the dear old sod
   Across the deep blue sea.

DERMOT'S FAREWELL.

Answer to 'You'll soon forget Kathleen.'

I can ne'er forget thee, Kathleen,
  Thou wilt still be dear to me,
My foot may rove a foreign land,
  My heart will dwell with thee.
Those happy hours with thee I pass'd
  I never can forget,
And though we're doomed by fate to part,
  I leave thee with regret.
Then dry thy tears, my Kathleen,
  O   more upon me smile,
And I soon return to thee, love,
  And the sunny Emerald Isle.

Strange faces cannot sever
  Our thoughts from those we love.
Ah! vain 'tis thy endeavor,
  True hearts they cannot move;
Above them all, a brighter spell,
  Is o'er our native home,
A charm that binds the heart there still,
  Where'er the foot may roam.
Then weep no more, my Kathleen,
  Once again upon me smile,
And I'll soon return to thee, love,
  And the sunny Emerald Isle.

TERRY MALONE.

One ev'ning from market returning,
Just thinking of what I'll not name;
May-be some of ye guess, ah! now don't ye
For 'tis few have not thought of the same.

But my heart is as open as sunshine,
A secret lies heavy as stone;
So I'll even confess, without blushing,
I was thinking of Terry Malone.

If you spake of some one I'll not mention,
It is certain, they say, he'll appear,
And so of the lad I was thinking,
By the bosheen I saw him draw near.

I was pleased yet sorry to see him,
And he asked me to meet him alone;
For I very well knew what he wanted,
So avoided poor Terry Malone.

Coming home the next ev'ning quite lonely,
All at once who d'ye think I did spy:
But Terry himself in a flurry,
And oh! such a beam in his eye!

Where's the use to descend to partic'lars,
Enough if the end be made known—
That same night, by the moon, I consented,
To become Mistress Terry Malone.

CASEY'S WHISKEY.

Words and Music by Joseph P. Skelly.

The Music of this song is published by E. H. Harding, 229 Bowery, New York. Price 10 cents.

Meself and Barney Casey wint to have a little spree,
He had a bottle for himself, and another one for me ;
We thravell'd round the city till our heads and feet were sore,
And ev'ry dhrink it was so nice, it made us wish for more.

CHORUS.

Bad luck to Casey's whiskey, it made us both so frisky,
We dhrank our bottles empty, and at last we couldn't stand ;
Along the streets we rambled, we staggered and we scrambled,
And sang a song, the whole night long, of gay ould Paddy's
land.

We met a big policeman, and he looked at us, says he,
"What brings you out so late as this?" says I, "the counthry's
free ;"
"Shut up," says Casey, "come along !" "O, divil a bit," says I,
"I'll sthrike him if he says a word, the durty mane ould spy."

Spoken —And if I ever did sthrike him he might well say—
                                    Bad luck to, etc.

He turned around and left us—sure the man was not to blame,
I called him back, and axed him if he'd plase to tell his name ;
"Of coorse," says he, "it's Flanigan, I'm from the county
Clare."
"Hurroo!" says I, "shake hands, me b'y, our whiskey you must
share !"
                                    Bad luck to, etc.

Out kem the empty bottle, and I put it in his paw,
"Look out," say he, "whin on me post, a dhrink's against the
law."
He put the bottle to his mouth, but divil a dhrop was there,
And while we laughed at Flanigan, sure he began to swear !
                                    Bad luck to, etc.

He raised his club above his head, and vow'd he'd take us in
For dhrinking on the highway, "O," says Casey, "that's too
thin !"
He dhragged poor Casey off to jail, and thried to take me too,
But to keep a hoult on Casey was as much as he could do.

Spoken.—I pitied poor Casey and I suppose he pitied me.
But it was all his own doings. The two bottles fixed him.
                                    Bad luck to, etc.

THE CHAP IN NUMBER NINE.

By J. B MURPHY.   Sung by JOHNNY WILD.

FOLKS wonder why I look so glum and seldom show my face,
As once I did, a year ago, in every public place ;
But they don't know how my poor heart was shivered up so fine,
By him that lives across the street—the chap in No. 9.

CHORUS.

My heart is broke—I nearly choke—when thinking of the time,
That Sarah Glass—run off, alas—with the chap in No. 9.

I'll tell you simply how it was and how it came to pass :
I loved a chambermaid next door, her name was Sarah Glass ;
I thought her soul a mirror pure—reflecting truth to mine,
Tho' oft she flashed a smile upon the chap in No. 9.

My heart is broke, etc.

I took Miss Glass to operas, balls, and every brilliant place,
And doated on her crystal eyes and clear, transparent face ;
I bought her gems of sparkling hue and presents rare and fine,
And dreamed of her and future bliss, nor thought of No. 9.

My heart is broke, etc.

At length the wished-for time was fixed to join our fates for life.
When Sarah Glass should ease my *pains* and be my darling wife ;
I danced and sang all day with joy, such bliss I can't define,
Nor envied once the fortunes of the chap in No. 9.

My heart is broke, etc.

Alas ! upon the very day that we were to be wed,
My hopes were shattered—Sarah Glass cleared out, vamoosed
    and fled ;
Her vows as brittle as her name, she broke with full design,
She sloped—run off—got—went—with the chap in No. 9.

My heart is broke, etc.

And now the dark and dismal hours in loneliness I pass,
Like some deserted picture-frame, forsaken by my glass ;
Life's bitter goblet thus I drain and not a hope is mine,
For they were smashed to pieces by the chap in No. 9.

My heart is broke, etc.

ALL THE WORLD AROUND.

IRISH NATIONAL SONG.

Words by T. D. SULLIVAN.   Music by SIR R. P. STEWART.

Where is love for Ire-land, Firm and fond and

true? Love that does not wav-er, Love that fal-ters

nev-er, Love that glows for-ev-er, As true

love should do. Here a-mong her chil-dren,

Here on I-rish ground, And near and far, 'neath

Chorus.

sun and star, All the world a-round. All the world a-

round, my boys, All the world a-round; By land and

sea, wher-e'er they be, All the world a-round.

(1)

ALL THE WORLD AROUND.—[Concluded.]

Where are prayers for Ireland,
  Breathed soft and low—
Earnest prayers and tender,
Asking God to send her
Peace and joy and splendor,
  Ending all her woe ?
They are heard wherever
  Ireland's sons are found,
From snow-clad lands to tropic sands,
  All the world around.

Cho.—All the world around, my boys,
    All the world around ;
    To heaven they rise, through all the skies,
    All the world around.

Where is aid for Ireland,
  If the need should be ?
If a foe oppress her,
If a wrong distress her,
Men who would redress her,
  Where shall Ireland see ?
Here, in crowds uncounted,
  Here such men are found,
And friends as true, not faint or few,
  All the world around.

Cho.—All the world around, my boys,
    All the world around ;
    Fond hearts and bold, she may behold,
    All the world around.

Yes, beloved Ireland,
  All so dear thou art,
Where young men, or hoary,
Tell of Brian's glory,
Where O'Neill's sad story
  Thrills through many a heart ;
Where Emmet's speech is spoken,
  Where Moore's sweet songs resound,
Where fond acclaim greets Grattan's name,
  All the world around.

Cho.—All the world around, my boys,
    All the world around ;
    There's help and cheer for Ireland dear.
    All the world around.

(2)

CAPT. KELLY'S MEDLEY.

HARK ! I hear an angel sing,
  In the cottage by the sea;
Give me back my wedding-ring,
  Sally is the girl for me.

Put me in my little bed,
  Where the foaming billows roll ;
I have not got nary red ;
  Johnny, come fill up the bowl.

Let me like a soldier fall,
  When the bloom is on the rye ;
Waiter, bring me one fish-ball,
  How is that, old boy, for high ?

Susey stole my heart from me,
  And she put it up the spout ;
Johnny's on another spree,
  That old thing is about played out.

Mary had a little sheep,
  Great on eating mutton-pies ;
Mother, I came home to sleep,
  Wake me up, when Kirby dies.

THE COT IN THE CORNER.

Song by Wm F. Sinclair Lawlor, in the laughable sketch of Barney
and the Ghost, as performed by Chas. Mac Evoy's original
Hibernicon Troupe.

Och hone, wirrastrew, how hard is our lot,
The landlord has turned us out of our cot,
To us in this world 'twas the happiest spot,
On the hill-side beyant in the corner ;
The roof was thatched over with bright yellow straw,
And the walls were as white as the snowflake agra,
Oh it was a fine picture a painter might draw,
From the boreen beyant in the corner.

It was purty without, it was tidy within,
On the shelves, shone like silver, our plate made of tin
Which cast some reflections when sunlight stole in,
On the dog and the cat in the corner ;
Of bacon, galore, we had many a flitch in
The wide mouthed chimney, that yawned in the kitchen,
Oh 'twould make your mouth water, and eager to pitch in
To the hames that hung high in the corner.

And there by the fire my mother would knit,
And close to her side my ould father would sit,
What stories he'd tell when his dudeen was lit,
While he smoked away in the corner;
When supper was over the neighbors dropped in,
And by the turf fire each roasted his shin,
While the boys and the girls ne'er thought it a sin
For to hug and to kiss in the corner.

When Jimmy the piper walked in on the floor,
The young people all made a rush for the door,
Dragging Jimmy along to the barn, and sure
They placed him high up in the corner ;
Then at it they went dear with hearts light and gay,
And danced the night hours into the young day,
'Till Jimmy got drunk an' no longer could play,
For he lay pipes and all in the corner.

THE BOLD IRISH SOLDIER.

AIR :—" Girl I Left Behind Me."

A raw recruit, och shure is me.
  I enlisted in Phildelaphy,
Field Marshal soon I came to be,
  Tip top of the Union army,
Oh, what pleasure an' oh what joys,
  'Twill be to gain promotion.
I've a taste for fighting' anyhow, boys,
  An' a better one for the lotion.

PATTER.

Arrah! an' ain't I, sure, fond of the lotion. Look at the bloom
on the top of my nose. Ain't it beautiful. But the worst of it
is it is always runnin' an' the divil a bit can I stop it, and that's
not military, is it lads? It wants a rum puncheon (punching). I
should think that would do it. But enough. I'll leave my nose
alone an' go on wid my tale. Well, afther I took the bounty, I
enlisted and got dhrunk to the tune of—

CHORUS.

With spirits gay I'll march away,
  All danger to be scorning;
I could fight all night till the break of day,
  An' come home quite fresh in the morning.

Now I an' another an' a good many more.
  Had to strip an' show our figure,
An' be well examined by Dr. O'Moore,
  Afore we could pull a trigger.
The Docther patted us on our backs,
  Say he, " None can be prouder,
Yez can give an' take some thunderin whacks,
  An' yer rattlin stuff for powder.

GET THE BEST! GET THE BEST!

There is just complaint among teachers and parents who take an interest in the culture of youth, because of the very few books that exist containing first class Dialogues for two or more speakers. Most of this class of books are mere repetitions of books printed scores of years ago; while others omit *all* old ones, however good, and fill their places with weak, wishy-washy pieces merely because they are *new*. In this series the aim has been to select *the Best*, whether new or old—pieces as fresh as daisies and as bright as stars.

MACAULAY'S
DIALOGUES ᶠᴼᴿ LITTLE FOLKS.

CONTAINING

A VERY LARGE NUMBER OF INTERESTING AND SPIRITED DIALOGUES, ON VARIOUS SUBJECTS, FOR FROM TWO TO TWENTY CHILDREN.

Some of these Dialogues are illustrations of the Seasons, Trades, Flowers, etc., and give an opportunity for a whole class to join in; and all of them give ample chance for the display of different degrees of natural ability and acquired proficiency. They afford faultless Parlor Entertainments, delightful to the young and pleasing to their friends.

This book contains 200 pages, bound in boards, with a brilliant, illuminated cover. **Price**...**50 Cents.**
A handsome and durable edition, bound in cloth, elegantly lettered in gilt. **Price**...**75 Cents.**

☞ *Copies of the above Book sent to any address in the world, postage paid, on receipt of price. Send Cash Orders to*

R. M. DE WITT, Publisher, 33 Rose st., N. Y.
(Between Duane and Frankfort sts.)

GET THE BEST! GET THE BEST!

The farmer thinks no pains ill-bestowed in preparing the soil and selecting his seed, if he wishes for a bountiful harvest. How much more necessary is it to give earnest attention to the minds of the Little Folks! The love of reading is now so universal that there is a demand on the part of parents and guardians for the Best Reading Books, and we have spared neither time nor expense in producing

WEBSTER'S
LITTLE FOLKS' SPEAKER.

COMPRISING

Many Standard Pieces, as well as a great many entirely original, both Sentimental and Humorous.

This book is one of the worthiest of its kind. It contains Two Hundred and Eleven Distinct Pieces, in Prose and Poetry, carefully selected from the best Authors, expressly for Reading and Recitation in Primary as well as the next grade of Public and Private Schools.

Not only is this work of very superior literary merit, but the printing and binding are models of neatness and strength.

A careful examination of Webster's Little Folks' Speaker will convince that every article has been carefully culled, and is marked by true morality as well as by excellence of diction. It can be placed in a child's hand with the certainty that the contents will improve the morals, as well as refine and cultivate the taste.

This book contains 200 pages, bound in board, with a brilliant, illuminated cover. Price... ....50 Cents.
A handsome and durable edition, bound in cloth, elegantly lettered in gilt. Price...75 Cents.

☞ *Copies of the above Book sent to any address in the world, postage free, on receipt of price. Send Cash Orders to*

R. M. DE WITT, Publisher, 33 Rose st., N. Y.

(Between Duane and Frankfort sts.)

64

Webster's Ready - Made Love Letters.

Comprising every style and kind of Note and Letter; from first acquaintance until marriage, from Ladies to Gentlemen, and from Gentlemen to Ladies. With details of the Customs and Etiquette of Courtship and Marriage. To which is added a complete Dictionary of Poetical Quotations, relative to Love, Courtship, and Marriage.
This book contains 200 pages, bound in boards, with elegantly illuminated cover...Price 50 Cents.
A very handsome edition, bound in cloth, elegantly lettered in gilt.
Price 75 Cents.

Napoleon's Complete Dream Book. Con-

taining Full, Plain and Accurate Explanations of Fortune-Telling by Dreams, Visions and Reveries. The only true and reliable Treatise (consulted by the Great Corsican) upon that most Useful and Marvellous Art. By MADAME CAMILLE LE NORMAND, the Modern Sibyl, Authoress of "Fortune-Telling by Cards," and other popular Treatises on the Occult Sciences.
This volume contains over 200 pages, bound in boards, with elegant illuminated cover...Price 50 Cents.
An elegant edition, bound in cloth, gilt lettered.......Price 75 Cents.

Fortune Telling by Cards; or, Cartomancy

Made Easy. Being a Pictorial and Practical Explanation of the marvellous Art of Prophetic Fortune-Telling, whereby through simple use of Single Head playing cards, any person of common intelligence can glean Full, Perfect, and Exact knowledge of the Past, the Present, and the Future.
This book contains over 200 pages, bound in boards, with a splendid illuminated cover ....Price 50 Cents.
A handsome and durable edition of this work, bound in cloth, elegantly lettered in gilt.....................................Price 75 Cents.

Note.—In trying fortunes by "Cartomancy Made Easy," it is necessary that a pack of cards should be used in which the face or figure cards have only a single head. We will furnish this style of card, of fine quality, for 75 Cents a pack, postage free.

Black Jokes for Blue Devils. Broad Grins

from Young Africa! Huge Guffaws from Sable Age! Wit from the Plantation! Wit from the Kitchen! Fun Ashore! Fun Afloat! Jokes in High and Low Life! Woolly Complications, conducive to loud laughter! A Book full and running over with side-splitting fun, "pecooliar " to the darkey'd race. Chock full of Colored Philosophy! Illustrated with 100 of the most Comic of all Comic Designs ever Engraved on Wood. Buy one copy of "Black Jokes for Blue Devils," containing a Thousand Comicalities, and near a Hundred Humorous Wood Cuts... Price 25 Cents.

The Swamp Outlaws; Or, The Lowery

Bandits of North Carolina. Large 8vo, eight illustrations.
Price 25 Cents.
The Carolina Bandits held far greater sway over the neighborhood of their swampy fastnesses than did Rob Roy over the Scottish Highlands, or Robin Hood over the English forests. Henry Berry Lowery, the leader, was a most extraordinary man, combining in his own person many of the qualities of the French Cartouche, and the Italian Rinaldi Ridaldini.

The Diseases of the Sexual System. By Dr.

EDWARD H. DIXON. Adapted to popular instruction.....Price $1.50
This eminent physician and surgeon clearly explains the structure, uses, abuses, and diseases of the most important organs of the human frame —not only important to the possessor, but doubly important as the means by which health and happiness, or disease and misery are transmitted to posterity. This book contains over 300 pages 12mo, well bound in cloth.

www.ingramcontent.com/pod-product-compliance
Lightning Source LLC
Chambersburg PA
CBHW021627270326
41931CB00008B/910